AF415317

# HELLA HOPEFUL:

## 31 Daily

# Affirmations

## to Find **Hope**

By: Kevin L. Marshall

# Dedication

To the memory of my friend, Officer Antwan Toney, thank you for your service and sacrifice. The memories of you give me hope that heaven is filled with admirable angels.

To the memory of my fraternity brother, Christopher Brient, your warmth and spirit shall transcend your presence on Earth. Thank you for blessing us with your warm smile; I still feel it each day.

To Rachel Pratt, my grandmother, thank you for answering the phone that dark summer night and giving me hope. I wouldn't be alive without you.

I pray that I have pleased each of you.

# Contents

# INTRODUCTION

Life is filled with beautiful, bright moments and trying, dark moments. I survive the dim moments by holding on to little pieces of light, and you can too. This book contains 31 daily affirmations, aimed at armoring you with hope to overcome even the toughest obstacles.

I would suggest reading one affirmation at the top of each day, meditating on the themes. These themes include love, strength, and self worth. As you read this book over the next 31 days, remember that hope should be a central theme. Convince yourself that with hope, anything is possible.

# Affirmation One: Hope and Love

God loves me. God loves me just the way I am. He loves me on my best days, and yes, even on my worst days. God created me just as I am. Nothing about me is a mistake. God knows the exact number of hairs on my head and designed each detail of my appearance and personality. God loves my skin tone, my hair, my eyes, my dialect, my accent, and even the way I dress. God loves everything about me. God loves me, and I will not allow the world to make me think any differently.

# Affirmation Two: Hope and Strength

I'm strong. Even when I feel weak and tired, I still have strength left. I am a conqueror; I can handle anything that's thrown at me. I'm powerful beyond measure and stronger than I realize. I will not give up in the face of adversity because I am strong. I'm a fighter. I have always been a fighter. I don't know how to back down from a fight. No matter what obstacles are thrown in my way, I have the strength to overcome them. I am so strong.

# Affirmation Three: Hope and Empowerment

I can do this. I believe in myself. I'm encouraged and empowered. God has equipped me with the necessary tools to make it through each day. I can do anything that I put my mind to. I can do all things through Christ who strengthens me. I can do this.

# Affirmation Four: Hope and Expectation

I have the expectation that something amazing will happen today. I truly believe that God has a miracle in store for me. I will continue to trust God, no matter how bad my situation looks. Each second is an opportunity for a miracle. I will spend today resting in the peace of expectancy.

# Affirmation Five: Hope and Worth

I deserve all of the blessings that God has for me. I will not be ashamed of what God has blessed me with. I will not apologize for the miracles in my life. I will embrace God's goodness and mercy. I deserve to be happy and celebrated. I deserve to smile, laugh, and love. I deserve it all.

# Affirmation Six: Hope and Freedom

I am unequivocally free. I will no longer live in the bondage of my past. I understand that my past experiences were used to mold and shape me, not to imprison me. I will not look back; I will focus on the future. Nothing in my past will stop me from moving forward.

God, thank you for freeing me. Thank you for allowing my experiences to shape my testimony. I am not in bondage. I am not a slave to any person, place, or thing. I am free in your will. I am free.

# Affirmation Seven: Hope and Beauty

I am beautiful. God created me in His image and designed me skillfully and intentionally. I take pride in knowing that I am special and unique. God did not make any mistakes when He made me.

I am confident on my own. I don't need the validation of others to feel beautiful. I will remind myself each day of how beautiful I am. I will continuously work on my inner and outer beauty, striving to be more physically, mentally, and spiritually attractive.

# Affirmation Eight: Hope and Progression

I have progressive thoughts; I will not look back. I cannot waste time ruminating on past decisions. There is nothing behind me; everything is in front of me. I will not live life in the rear-view mirror.

I will overcome past hurt, disappointment, and failure. Generational curses and chains are broken. Unhealthy relationships are a thing of the past. I welcome new people, goals, and experiences.

My mind creates innovative strategies and million-dollar ideas. My mindset is that of a leader and not a follower. I am strong enough to lead others, shape communities, and move this world forward.

# Affirmation Nine: Hope and Consistency

I am in a season of supernatural victories. In this season, I cannot lose. I refuse to accept defeat; nothing can keep me from success. This season will be filled with trophies and congratulations. God will release more blessings than I can handle.

# Affirmation Ten: Hope and Perfection

I don't have to be perfect. I am proud of myself, as long as I'm striving to be the best person that I can be. I take joy in each step towards progression; mistakes are merely lessons learned. The Lord has forgiven me for past mistakes, and I also forgive myself. Progress is my goal, not perfection.

# Affirmation Eleven: Hope and New Beginnings

Each day, I am blessed with an opportunity for a fresh start. It is up to me to take advantage of the clean slate. Today is a new day, filled with endless possibilities. Today, I will push myself in ways that I have not yet imagined. I will live life like it's the beginning and not the end. I will be present, live in the moment, and focus on today.

# Affirmation Twelve: Hope and Comfort

I am not lonely; I live in an abundance of love and comfort. God is shaping and preparing me for my better half. I trust that God has someone specifically designed to meet my needs. I rest easy knowing that God is always by my side and that I am never alone.

Each day, I am working to become the best version of myself. I am preparing to be a better husband, wife, or partner. I am not lonely -- I am growing.

# Affirmation Thirteen: Hope and Inspiration

I will inspire. I am a born leader with talent and influence. I have ideas that will inspire others; younger generations will look to me for example and wisdom. I will not be afraid to be who I truly am, as others will be inspired to follow suit. I will lead fearlessly, by example, and inspire others with my actions and opinions. I am an influencer. I will inspire.

# Affirmation Fourteen: Hope and Optimism

Today, I take control of my thoughts. I choose to starve negative thoughts and feed positive ones. I speak life into the universe and meditate on happiness. I'm optimistic that amazing things will happen for me. Each day, I have a choice of whether to be happy or sad. Each day, I will remember to choose happiness. I am not depressed; I am encouraged.

# Affirmation Fifteen: Hope and Legacy

I will change the world. I have the power to leave this world better than I found it. At birth, God equipped me with an assignment. My assignment will shape history. My legacy will forever be remembered.

# Affirmation Sixteen: Hope and Location

Favor follows me wherever I go. Blessings will chase after me for eternity. I will operate in abundance; my life will overflow with blessings. I will lack nothing. Blessings will locate me.

# Affirmation Seventeen: Hope and Happiness

Today, I take control of my thoughts. I will speak life into the universe and will invest in my happiness. I'm optimistic that amazing things will happen for me. Each day, I have a choice to be happy or to be sad. I choose happiness.

# Affirmation Eighteen: Hope and Value

I am valuable. I have options; I don't have to settle. I deserve the absolute best; and I won't settle for anything less than that. I'll wait forever if I have to. I deserve to be with someone who loves me and treats me with respect. I am not restricted or bound. There are always options.

I know my worth and will hold myself to the highest standards. I deserve loyalty, respect, and decency. I am more valuable than gold, and precious in the eyes of the Lord.

# Affirmation Nineteen: Hope and Promotion

God, I desire more than what I already have. I know your favor is endless. Enlarge my territory and advance me to the next level. Lord, I know your desires for my life exceed my own. Prepare my mind and heart for my next journey. Thank you in advance for your blessings and promotion.

# Affirmation Twenty: Hope and a Smile

No matter what obstacles are placed in my way today, I will take time to minister through my smile. A simple smile can change someone's day for the better. A smile can shift any atmosphere and cultivate positive vibrations. I will spread love and light throughout the day, remembering that there is always a reason to smile.

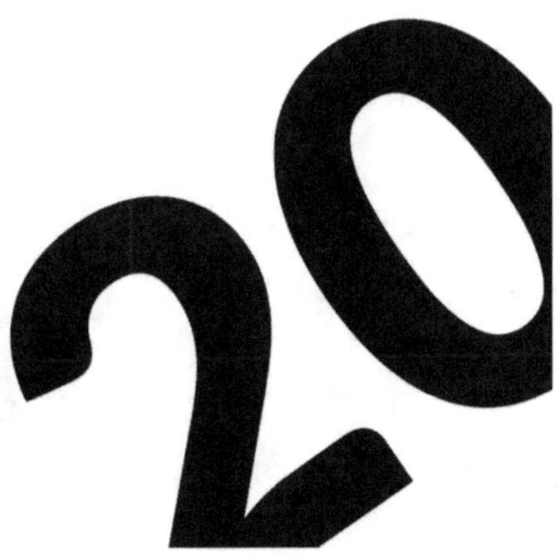

# Affirmation Twenty-One: Hope and Boundaries

I must set realistic boundaries and expectations for my relationships. Failing to set boundaries in friendships and intimate relationships can cause stress and chaos. Being mindful of personal boundaries is essential for my mental health and the healthiness of my relationships.

# Affirmation Twenty-Two: Hope and Salvation

God, I believe you sent your son Jesus Christ to die for my sins. Your word says that whoever believes in you will not perish, but have everlasting life. God, I acknowledge you as my savior; I trust you with my life. As time here on Earth shortens with each day, I rest assured knowing that I will spend eternity with you.

# Affirmation Twenty-Three: Hope and Focus

I am focused on my goals and dedicated to achieving my dreams. I will tenaciously pursue success in all areas of my life. I refuse to allow others to distract me from accomplishing my full potential; nothing can stand in my way. I awake each morning excited, knowing that I am one step closer to the finish line.

# Affirmation Twenty-Four: Hope and Patience

All of my hopes and desires are manifesting right before my eyes. Everything that I deserve will find me. God will provide all of my heart's desires; He has not forgotten about me. Everything that I desire is forthcoming, and I will wait patiently for my blessings.

# Affirmation Twenty-Five: Hope and Protection

God is protecting me, even when it seems like I'm in a difficult season. God is always by my side; He will never leave me. In life, tough times are inevitable. However, I will not allow tough times to defeat me. All storms must end at some point; there is sunshine on the other side of the clouds. No matter how things look, I know that light is on the way.

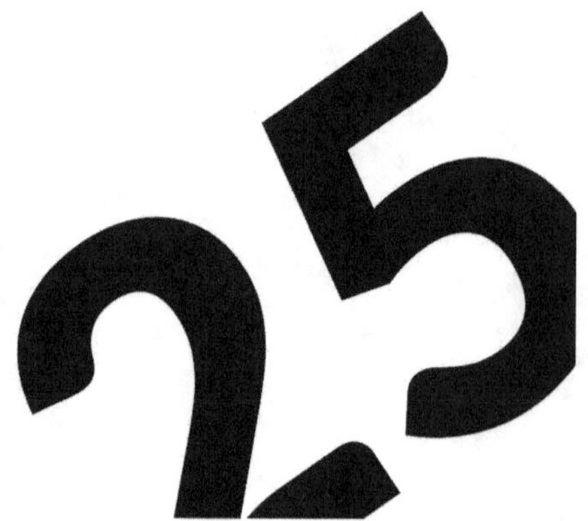

# Affirmation Twenty-Six: Hope and Survival

I am strong enough to overcome any obstacle placed in my way. I will survive this, just as I've survived hardships in my past. The Lord gives me strength when I am weak. God gives me peace and comfort when I am in need. I am never fighting alone, for He is always fighting by my side. I will survive.

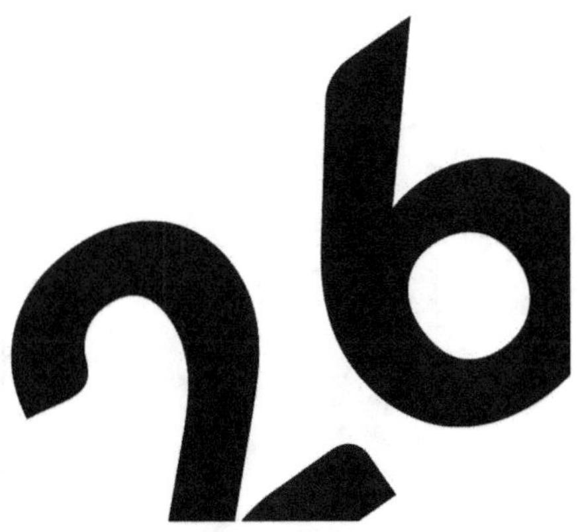

# Affirmation Twenty-Seven: Hope and Healing

God, thank you for healing me. Thank you for healing my body, my mind, my soul, and my spirit. I know that nothing is impossible for you. I trust you with my life, and I rest easy knowing that my health is in your precious hands. I know that you're working on my behalf, no matter how bad things may seem. God, you are a healer and I am healed.

# Affirmation Twenty-Eight: Hope and Safety

I admit that sometimes I'm afraid. I'm scared of the uncertainty that tomorrow brings. God, I understand that as your child, I should rest knowing that you will keep me safe. You are always there for me, no matter what obstacles I may face. I rest assured knowing that I am always protected under your watchful eye. You will never leave me; I am never alone.

# Affirmation Twenty-Nine: Hope and Triumph

I am strong enough to overcome any obstacle placed in my way. Past mistakes do not define me; nothing can stop me. Each day, I will take advantage of the opportunity for a fresh start. I will live in each moment, and let go of the past. I can come back from anything; there is nothing that can immobilize me.

# Affirmation Thirty: Hope and Uniqueness

I will never be ashamed of my differences. My differences empower me. God designed me as I am, and I'm beautiful inside and out. I am perfect, and my differences make me unique.

# Affirmation Thirty-One: Hope and Abundance

God has not forgotten about me. God has heard each of my prayers, and He will answer all of them. God will provide all of my needs. His love for me is indescribable and cannot be measured. No matter how hard life may seem, my season of abundance is approaching. No one can stop the forthcoming blessings.

9 798640 722727